The Great Totnes Book

Chips Barber
with Bill Bennett MBE

Illustrations by
Jane Reynolds

*First published in 1990, Reprinted in 1991, 1992, 1996, 2002 and 2006 by
Obelisk Publications, 2 Church Hill, Pinhoe, Exeter, Devon
Designed by Chips and Sally Barber
Edited and Typeset by Sally Barber
Printed in Great Britain by
Avocet Press, Cullompton, Devon*

Totnes is a town in South Devon with a population of about 6,000. The small size of the town belies its enormous reputation, for it is a place well known throughout the kingdom and, if the ever-flowing current of foreign visitors continues, it will be well known throughout the world. And rightly so, because Totnes is a unique place with a special atmosphere: hard to relate in words, but, hopefully, easier to communicate in visual terms.

Most visitors to the town arrive from the direction of Torbay, and have to exercise extreme patience when joining the inevitable traffic queue that forms down Bridgetown Hill. There seems to be a distinct pattern – the greyer and duller the day, the longer the queue! However, on arrival in Totnes all is soon forgotten and the throng of visitors forms an impressive tide of humanity rising up or drifting down the steep main street.

This little guide book aims to provide an attractive and informative souvenir of your visit, or even acquaintanceship, with this ancient Devon borough. It is a town whose history goes back through the ages – possibly to the times of the Romans, who might have been borne up the Dart on a strong tide. Certainly there is evidence to suggest some sort of Roman presence, as a number of old coins have been found in the district. In far off Stockholm, at the Royal Cabinet of Antiquities, some 21 coins, minted in Totnes during the Anglo-Saxon era, are housed in a collection; there are also coins of this period on exhibition at the Totnes Guildhall and Museum. However, it is unlikely that the early settlement would have had more than a few hundred people at most.

This little book is not simply a history book, but will try to give you an impression of what Totnes is all about. By the time you have read about some of its triumphs and failures, been introduced to its personalities and places, you will begin to appreciate why it is such a revered town. As you negotiate its narrow streets and see its charming and unusual shops, you will start to sense and feel some of its magic. The first section of the book starts at Totnes Bridge and ascends the Fore Street, struggles up the High Street and pokes around some of the back streets at the top of the town. The second section is primarily concerned with the waterfront and the flat bits of what is one of Devon's hilliest towns. The last section visits those celebrated venues on the outskirts of Totnes, the parts that all visitors should reach in their Totnes time. The drawings include past and present pictures, but who knows what the future holds for Totnes?

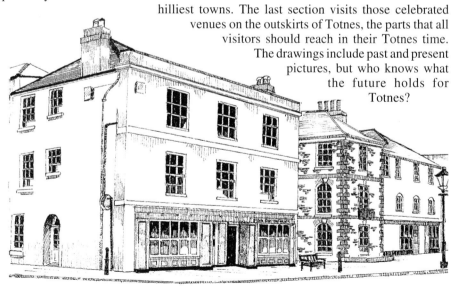

Our first port of call is on the right hand side of the Fore Street and has been a popular watering place for several centuries. The Royal Seven Stars has more than one claim to fame with a history dating back to 1660. This was the same year that Daniel Defoe, author of *Robinson Crusoe* and *Moll Flanders,* was born. He stayed here in 1720 whilst exploring this part of the world, gathering information and making observations for his book *A Tour through the Whole Island of Great Britain,* published in 1724. In his 71 years he wrote some 500 journals, pamphlets and books. It is recorded that Defoe was charged a shilling for a fine salmon dinner, the fish having been taken at the bridge immediately outside the hostelry. Being the son of a butcher he greatly enjoyed his food. He made the observation that Totnes was an inexpensive place in which to dine. As he had spent two or three years in Newgate Prison, a stay in somewhere as well-provisioned as the Seven Stars must have been greatly appreciated.

The record books show that the inn was important in the days of the stage coach. In 1823 several coaches left the Seven Stars each day to head for

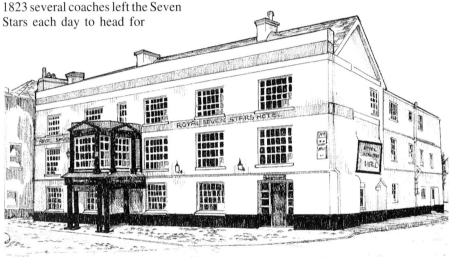

London and a host of other destinations. Its popularity with well-to-do persons ensured its reputation spread far and wide; Edward VII, George V, Edward VIII, George VI and present male members of the Royal family, as Cadets on the Britannia at Dartmouth, have all been clients, hence the prefix 'Royal'.

The Hotel has worn many different functional hats. Apart from the obvious purpose for which it was built, it has acted as a cinema and a theatre and has hosted many lavish balls and dances. Joe Tapley ran film shows in the ballroom during the early 1920s, before moving up the road to 27 Fore Street where he converted his property into a modern cinema. The first 'talkie' film shown here was *Dark Red Roses*, but during the last war the cinema was destroyed by a fire, which started in the auditorium, depriving the town of a much-treasured amenity. During the First World War army officers were taken to the Seven Stars for convalescence. The Totnes air, the beauty of the Dart, and the excellent fayre of the hotel helped rehabilitate many men. But there is far more to see in Totnes and, unlike Defoe's most famous character, Robinson Crusoe, we must not get 'marooned' with our memories at the Seven Stars. The hill of Fore Street is quite gentle at this point; it is possible to appreciate the architectural features of the buildings that line both sides of the street.

A building of outstanding architecture is the Mansion built in 1795. In 1887 the Totnes Grammar School, founded by Edward VI in 1553, moved from the Guildhall precinct to here. When the late Alec Clifton-Taylor presented a TV programme about Totnes, he did an excellent job in relating the varied architecture although he didn't bare its soul. He was, however, critical of the ivy growing on this building and his televised disgust was instrumental in its removal.

Many of the former pupils of the school have achieved public acclaim for their works. Edward Lye (1704–67) was the compiler and author of an Anglo-Saxon and Gothic Dictionary, which was published after his death. Another literary former fellow of the school was Dr Benjamin Kennicott (1718–83) who collated all the existing Hebrew versions of the Old Testament, and, in 1772, published them together for the first time, so that scholars could compare them.

However, Professor Clifton-Taylor was appreciative of the Strawberry Hill Gothic designed building that is nearby. It has the unusual distinction of having a public right of way pass through it. Many people pass by without noticing its fine architecture – probably because it is set a little way back from the street.

On the opposite side, and just below the former Grammar School, is the former Post Office. This attractive building, which was completed in June 1928, has a face and roof hung with slate from the world-famous Delabole Quarry in Cornwall.

It is worth keeping an eye out for Atherton Lane, one of the narrowest of side streets, which has plaques at the entrance proclaiming that it has been the 'best kept' in a South Hams town twice during the 1980s.

As the hill becomes much steeper, one of the town's most celebrated features, the Brutus Stone, is found on the right hand side of Fore Street, just above number 51. The reason for specifying this precise point is that many people walk right past without seeing it. Legend has it that this humble, but important, stone is the very first stone that Brutus the Trojan set foot on when he came ashore. For all good "Brits" the significance lies in the wayward belief that Britain takes its name from this legendary coloniser. A little rhyme supports his enthusiasm:

"Here I stand and here I rest
And this good town shall be called Totnes."

And indeed it was – but not quite like that. The story, which has been nurtured, distorted, enlivened and enriched by Totnesians, goes on to tell how Brutus was the son of Aeneas the Trojan who, after killing his father in a hunting accident, mounted his horse and set off to Greece with an army of followers. He defeated the Greek king and married his daughter, then, on the advice of the oracle of Diana, set sail to Britain. Whilst at Totnes he valiantly took on and defeated many giants. Despite the dubious origin of stories surrounding it, the Brutus Stone has an important place in Totnes's tradition and history, as it is used for important Royal proclamations.

Another veritable treasure not to be missed is Totnes Museum, housed at No 70, which is on the left hand side of Fore Street just below the East Gate. A visit is a 'must', rain or shine! It is not at all surprising to note that Totnes Museum has won many accolades, you have to spend only a few hours here to appreciate its great charms. It is an Elizabethan house, which dates back to about 1575; whilst various fires have often raged through compact Totnes causing great damage, this house has thankfully survived. The building came on the market in 1958 and the Totnes Borough Council were enthusiastically convinced, by various local persons, that such a gem of architectural heritage should not be lost: by 1961 Totnes Museum had evolved. The work of dedicated craftsmanship over three years for its superb restoration, is to be commended.

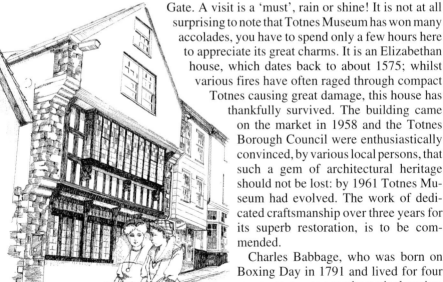

Charles Babbage, who was born on Boxing Day in 1791 and lived for four score years, was a mathematical genius. Although not born here, his family were true Totnesians; his grandfather was the Mayor of Totnes in 1754 and his father was an influential and wealthy banker.

The Great Little Totnes Book

Totnes Grammar School, which was then adjoining Totnes Guildhall, gave Charles the educational foundation needed to secure a place at Trinity College, Cambridge. Charles was an eccentric, but highly popular, character. On one occasion he tried, with the aid of wooden paddles, to walk across the River Dart! Needless to say his design specifications were not quite up to it and the poor chap nearly drowned after a few hesitant, wobblingly precarious seconds. Despite this appliance of science being a failure, Charles used his immense mathematical capacity well and throughout the world was held in the highest esteem.

He used some of his personal fortune to help fund a lifetime's venture in attempting to create a mechanical form of mathematical computation. He experimented with various machines, but his 'Analytical Engine' was one of the most ambitious projects he undertook. Using punch cards the machine could automatically solve algebraic equations; from various accounts it is apparent that Charles' great genius led him to the brink of creating something which could be compared with the first electronic computers. However, Charles lived at a time when other factors were against him, and for various reasons his brainchild was never fully assembled.

Sadly, Babbage died before fulfilling his dreams, a somewhat bitter and disappointed man, obviously generations ahead of his time, whose last few years were spent battling against the organ grinders who played outside his home, greatly inconveniencing him in his mathematical meditations. As is often the case, it was only after his death that his true genius was fully appreciated. When the popular television quiz series *Family Fortunes* first appeared, host Bob Monkhouse used to call the computer 'Mr Babbage'! More importantly, in recognition of Babbage's mathematical achievements, International Computers have presented Totnes Museum with a fine exhibition on his life and varied achievements.

The next stop is at the landmark that features in every photographic representation of Totnes – the East Gate – one of two surviving gates, the other being the North. Owned by the Duke of Somerset, this fine arch was destroyed by fire in September 1990, but has since been faithfully rebuilt at huge expense.

A short distance above this famous arch is one of the reddest churches in Devon. The parish church of St Mary's is a little way above the East Gate arch and is a major landmark; its distinctly red 120-foot sandstone tower can be seen from many viewpoints around the immediate landscape. It is a place of peace, of sanctuary and of great beauty. The organ, which can play a mighty note, was part of the huge organ built for the Great Exhibition of 1851, which was to signify a reign of peace. Escaping from the hustle and bustle of an often busy main street, it is possible to sit and savour some of St Mary's treasures. The magnificent stone rood screen is regarded as the finest in Devon and probably one of the best in England. In 1459 Beer stone was bought around the coast from East Devon and up the Dart for its construction; this was by order of the corporation so that the chancel should be separated from the church just like at Exeter Cathedral. The sandstone for the church was probably quarried in the Paignton area, a rich source for this typically Devonian stone. It is believed that the design of the church tower is based on four other West Country towers. Town worthies visited Ashburton, Buckland Monachorum, Tavistock and Callington

and were no doubt so inspired by what they observed that the fine Totnes tower embodies what is best in the design of these churches.

It is always rather incongruous to see a sundial in Devon, a county which has more than its fair share of cloud and rain at the best of times – the benefactor of such an object either has a keen sense of humour, or is a fervent optimist. However, there is one on the south west wall of Totnes Church. This was paid for by Edward Windeatt as a memorial to his brother, T. T. Windeatt who died, aged 58, in 1903. Edward felt that his brother had served the town well in many capacities – as a solicitor, churchwarden and Mayor. As part of the inscription it gives the latitudinal and longitudinal co-ordinates of the position of the sundial. Sited at 50° 26" North and 3° 4" West the sundial, placed in 1904, is a perpetual memorial to a man who had a keen interest in Totnes's affairs. No doubt this was a family trait as Edward too was an excellent literary recorder of the town's history and heritage; this little book would be much the poorer for its content but for gleaning goodies from his research.

However, when the sun is high, in the glory of a warm Totnes day, do not be tempted to trust in the shadow cast across the sundial; if you are about to catch a train, boat or plane, you must remember that 'Totnes Time' is just over 12 minutes behind Greenwich Mean Time, because Totnes is to the west of London and the sun therefore is directly overhead a little later than in the capital!

In recent years there has been a trend, at popular tourist haunts, to attempt to recapture the flavour of the past. Shaldon, opposite Teignmouth, has a '1785 day' on Wednesdays throughout the summer, St Marychurch has a Victorian Day and at Morwellham Quay in the Tamar Valley, miners, maidens and maritime men dress in Victorian costume to celebrate the heyday of that place. However, Totnes can proudly boast that they were well ahead of their time, whilst at the same instance going well back into it. Since 1970 many Totnes traders and townsfolk have donned glamorous Elizabethan costumes to add great gaiety and colour to Totnes's summer Tuesdays.

The choice of period is most appropriate, as Totnes was at its peak of importance when it was a thriving Elizabethan town – after that time other Devon towns became relatively more important. Many fine Elizabethan edifices remain to create a most appropriate backcloth, and the characters in the costumes are as colourful in their personalities as in their dress! Through the years the 'Elizabethans' have raised a great amount of money for a variety of charities, and there is perhaps no better way of savouring the delights of Totnes than by going on an afternoon guided walk with one of them.

Whilst every summer Tuesday is an Elizabethan extravaganza, there is one special event held in July that particularly merits a mention, commemorating that most famous of Elizabethans Sir Francis Drake, and an orange! The story goes that Sir Francis often visited Totnes, and, on one occasion, being 'all fingers and thumbs', he dropped a basket of oranges at the top of the steep main street and watched helplessly as they rolled all the way to the bottom of the town. Another version simply states that Sir Francis presented an orange to a little Totnes lad called Robert Hayman, who later qualified in law and went on to become Governor of Newfoundland. Robert Hayman's hobby was poetry (he had many published) and he wrote of Drake:

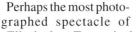

"This man when I was little, I did meet
As he was walking up Totnes long street.
He asked me whose I was? I answered him.
He asked me if his good friends were within?
A faire red orange in his hand he had,
He gave it me where of I was right glad..."

In 1978 the Elizabethan Society instigated a race to commemorate the event. Initially the object of the exercise was for the participants to roll an orange down the entire length of the street without damaging the fruit, but in more recent times the activity has become more of a race than an exercise in citric conservation!

Perhaps the most photographed spectacle of Elizabethan Totnes is the popular ritual of visitors installing themselves in a well-constructed set of stocks to pose for the obligatory snapshot – Man at his most vulnerable. Behind this stock joke is the Elizabethan market, with its surfeit of stalls, most of which sell locally made items ranging from honey to handicrafts.

This site has seen a procession of buildings come and go. The original market hall was called The Shambles, but it was replaced by a new one in 1848. This lasted precisely a century before extensive renovation work created a new public hall. Unfortunately, fire, so often a menace in Totnes, gutted this edifice in 1955. The current building is the Civic Hall, which has survived since 1960, within which are markets, providing yet another venue where some unusual items can be purchased.

So far we have neglected to mention Totnes's shops, but anyone who is observant will have noticed that there is a distinct lack of chain stores and multiples. Therefore, almost every shop is a 'one-off', an individual trader, which makes for an interesting shopping expedition; combined with the friendly personal approach, this personifies the charm of Totnes.

Although common in Europe, piazzas or Butterwalks are less familiar adornments to the English landscape. However, downstream, Dartmouth has some excellent examples which date back to about 1628, possibly inspired by the earliest efforts constructed at Totnes in 1584. Many of Totnes's Butterwalks or Poultry walks were added during the eighteenth century. Frequently a Tudor rear was masked by a Georgian façade! The additional frontage was achieved by supporting the projected building with piers at the corners. Occasionally these were timber supports, but the durability of

stone usually prevailed. It is easy to imagine the country traders operating with great enthusiasm in a shaded location where the butter, cream, cheese, eggs and poultry remained in a more saleable condition than in the bright light and heat of a summer's day. Alas, the shopkeepers were not so enthused by the vendors beneath these piazzas, and in time they were prohibited from bawling out their wares on the pavement. The added amenity of extra living space, gained by the projection over the street, had to be paid for and an annual fee for 'encroachment' was charged for such a privilege.

The close knit nature of Totnes's shops and houses and the amount of timber in them means that fire is a greater threat to the town than in many other places. There have been many scares in past years. At the end of January 1903 a draper's store at 40–42 High Street, opposite the Butterwalk, caught alight one Saturday evening. The flames were fanned by a very strong wind, which intensified the problem so much that the Paignton Fire Brigade was sent for and a telegraph sent to both Plymouth and Exeter for additional help. Fortunately for the town the wind suddenly dropped and the supply of water held out long enough to dowse the flames.

Just along the road, fire destroyed the Commercial Hotel in 1930, but another more serious conflagration broke out in March 1931. The premises at 58 High Street, Messrs. Distin, caught alight and the ensuing fire forced the Mayor, James Palmer, to race back to the town as fast as he could. It was not a case of civic concern on his part, though – it was *his* premises that were alight! Coincidentally, he was actually involved in starting a fire at the time – he was 'swaling' the heathland a few miles from Chagford, an act designed to improve and encourage new growth in grazing areas. Unfortunately there was not much he could do, and a great deal of damage was done to his property. It was noted on this occasion that the town's water supply was inadequate to deal with this scale of disaster.

Although the waters of Totnes might have been insufficient in volume to dowse fires, at least they were of a quality to effect various cures. The Leechwells are to be found down a lane leading off Leechwell Street near the Kingsbridge Inn. The way to them is clearly signposted, and a visit is worthwhile. They consist of three stone baths or sinks, which are fed by three jets of water coming out of holes in the adjacent wall. These curative waters have flowed for many centuries, and each supply has its own peculiar name. Depending on your medical problem, be it snake

bite, skin disease or blindness, you could sample the waters from troughs called 'Snake', 'Toad' or 'Long Crippler' (this being dialect for a slow worm or blind worm). There was nothing unusual about waters like this being used for effecting cures – at nearby Ashburton, St Gudula's Well was also known for its usefulness in alleviating eye disorders. The only real problem with the Leechwells seemed to be demand – at the time when they were at their most efficacious, there wasn't enough water to satisfy it.

However, today they are seldom used and most visitors to this part of the town seem to prefer the 'waters' of the Kingsbridge Inn at the top of the lane. This is believed to be the oldest inn in the town, partly fourteenth century, and has a deceptively spacious interior. Its reputation for good fayre, and its pleasant atmosphere, make it the perfect oasis in which to pause awhile before continuing a look around Totnes.

For the purposes of this book this is about as far up the town as we'll go.

On returning towards the main part of the town, the distinctive keep of Totnes Castle stands out above the roof tops. In the summer season the castle is open to the public, and a short climb leads to the top from where there is a lovely view. If you peer over the numerous interlocking roof tops of the town, which lies at the foot of the castle, you may glimpse the distant sheet of water that is the Dart. If you look towards Dartmoor, such landmarks as Buckland Beacon and Rippon Tor, the highest point on the eastern side, are visible. (However, if you were to stand on Rippon Tor, it would be no easy matter trying to pinpoint Totnes Castle, which, from the moor, appears tucked over the shoulder of Dartington's great hill.)

North Gate

Although it was the Saxons who first developed the site of the town, it was not until Norman times that the impressive stone circular keep appeared in the landscape. William granted the Manor of Totnes to Juhel, or Judhael, who made Totnes his chief residence. He chose a site at the north-west end of the borough. Alas, in 1088–89 he was deprived of his lands for his part in a rebellion; his possessions, which included a hundred manors, were given to Roger de Nonant.

Today there are various remains to see. There is the motte or mound that rises over fifty feet from the bailey below; this is crowned by the perfectly circular stone keep with walls 15 feet thick. The inner bailey or court was surrounded by a deep moat and encircled by a wall. Much of this is still to be seen, but there is no water in the moat. A large company of men and horses, along with all their stores, could have been easily accommodated here. There were also a chapel and a large hall within the bailey.

The Great Little Totnes Book

The castle endured fluctuating fortunes. In the fifteenth century it had fallen into disuse, but was occasionally used as an administrative centre for the affairs of the town – the Assize of Bread and Ale took place here; for privileges such as these, the tenants did duty to the Lord of the Manor.

During the English Civil War (1642–46) Totnes changed hands many times without a great deal of fighting. It has been noted by many historians that the local population fared far worse than the troops. It didn't seem to matter whether the Roundheads or Royalists were in town, as both sides relied on the local populace for their food. When the war ended things didn't improve – the Plague visited the town causing the deaths of 262 people within a short period; the streets became so deserted that grass and weeds grew in the main street, and the castle became a very sad and neglected spectacle.

In 1931 visitors to Totnes who wanted to visit the castle had to pay sixpence to go in, but first they had to go and collect the key "from the house on the further side of the street opposite"!

Totnes's other ancient building, the Guildhall, is not far away and lies just to the north, or behind, St Mary's Church. For centuries the wise men of Totnes have met and deliberated over matters of importance and occasionally more parochial. The Guildhall granite pillars or octagonal piers seem such a natural, integral part of the building, but they originally stood at the Merchant's Exchange of 1616 in the High Street. This was demolished in 1878 (Bradford & Bingley's now stands on the site) and to waste such fine columns of Dartmoor granite would have been a shame, so some were erected at the Guildhall, which was then given a more distinct and distinguished appearance.

In 1945 a film was made called *I Live in Grosvenor Square*, which starred such well known names as Rex Harrison, Robert Morley and Anna Neagle. They filmed an 'election' scene below the church wall and outside of the Guildhall. Alas, for one reason or another there were problems, so they recreated,

at Elstree studios, an exact replica of the scene, both inside and outside of this wonderful old building. Some of the local Totnes folk who had been involved were invited up to London for a re-take, and were flabbergasted at the re-creation: it was so good they thought they were back at the real thing! The full story of this, and other amusing stories concerning films and television programmes filmed in the county, is told in my book *Made in Devon.*

The Guildhall is an ancient building that, until 1962, possessed positively no sanitary arrangements. The only facilities until that time were for men only, and were the sort only men would use, being nothing more sophisticated than a vertical wall adjoining the Guildhall! The alarm bells rang when it became known that the Queen was going to visit the Guildhall for more than a few fleeting moments. It was duly decreed that the necessary plumbing arrangements be made and a 'throne room' was accordingly added. However, somebody observed that the men's flushing system was so noisy that it might well constitute a right royal disturbance, so that too was put before the privy council and was duly sorted out. The Royal visit went smoothly, the main purpose being to open a new cattle market.

Anyone coming back to Totnes after an absence of many years will be amazed at the changes that have taken place on the elegant street which is called 'The Plains', a thoroughfare running parallel to the River Dart. It has been given a new lease of life, transformed from a twilight zone of disused warehouses to an area brimming with new residences and businesses.

Many years ago there were two companies manufacturing cider on The Plains: Bentall, Lloyd and Co and Symons and Co. The latter also made wine and had their 'fruit mills' in the town. They had a nationwide reputation and their advertising helped to put Totnes on the map, showing an elderly smocked local raising a glass of cider, with an invitation to call in at Totnes to sample their considerable range of ciders. Another company, Bowden and Coombes, produced their cider at a magnificent warehouse called the Blue Ball, near to South Street, which has since been converted into flats.

At the beginning of The Plains is an obelisk with an Antipodean connection. The Wills Monument stands a short distance from Totnes Bridge. It is a fine monument that reflects a most colourful, but tragic, story of a Totnesian who was born but a stone's-throw away from it. William J. Wills was born in 1834, the son of a local doctor. His father believed that his two sons would make a better life if they went to Australia, so, after all the necessary arrangements had been made, in 1852 they were duly dispatched there. Work had been found for William in an Australian goldfield, but he disliked the rough, tough conditions and sought a more genteel environment. Fortune smiled on him, and he acquired a post as an astronomer and meteorologist at an observatory in Melbourne. His diverse abilities and undoubted skills were soon recognised, and in 1860 he was engaged as a surveyor for an expedition attempting to cross the hitherto little explored interior of Australia. The principal aim was to reach the Gulf of Carpentaria using an inland route.

The chosen leader of the expedition was a man called Burke, rather aptly named as he was prone to make rash judgments, and, worse, was a man dogged by bad luck – not the sort of qualities one would appreciate when setting out on so precarious an expedition! Robert O'Hara Burke was an intrepid Irishman who had been born in Galway in 1820. In Australia he had become a police inspector on the goldfields of Victoria. The group of seventeen set out from Victoria, but at their first objective, Cooper's Creek, Burke sent about half back to the start to get extra supplies. He left another three members of the party at Cooper's Creek, and with Wills, two assistants and six camels, set off across the vast continental interior. Success was achieved as the expedition reached the Gulf of Carpentaria in February 1861.

It was Burke's bad luck that in one of the driest places on all the earth, the returning expeditioners had to endure heavy continuous rain. The weather was so inclement, and

conditions were so bad, that one of the party died. They were then severely delayed and got back to Cooper's Creek late on the same day that the 'supply' camp had just left. Further misfortunes then followed as Burke led his companions into the hot desert, and a lingering death. Wills was found with his diary left open beside him, his last few entries dramatically chronicling his plight and recounting his desperate bid to survive. However, there was a survivor, a man called King, who held on long enough to be rescued by Aborigines. The bodies of Burke and Wills were brought back to Melbourne, and their great pioneering efforts were reflected in the way in which they lay in state for almost three weeks before being buried amid much pomp and ceremony. There have been further tributes to them, including a monument near Australia House in London, and another in Melbourne. There is a town called Burketown near the coast on the Gulf of Carpentaria, and, slightly less impressively, two roads on the industrial estate in Totnes have been named Burke Road and Wills Road. The Wills Monument in Totnes is visited by many Australians each year.

In the 1986 Australian film version of this epic journey, Nigel Havers played the part of Wills, with Jack Thompson in the role of Burke.

Although Totnes's main thoroughfare is the steep main street, The Plains provides a far less claustrophobic or crowded environment. This was the business end of the town, and in its trading heyday was a colourful, highly industrial scene. A railway line led from Totnes Station all the way down to the various quays along the Dart. But now the tide of trade has turned and the area is becoming occupied by some fairly upmarket residential and shopping developments.

Opposite the Wills Monument is a group of fine looking buildings. A locally set up

Preservation Trust has carefully and superbly restored them. For a number of years, the National Trust Shop was housed in a 1710 brick building believed to be a former Georgian Merchant's house, which had all but collapsed. The brick front had to be completely rebuilt, and it has been done so that access has been created through to the old Town Quay, which lies behind it. The redeveloper thought that to do this would make it more of a fun building, as people enjoy milling around courtyards and along lanes. The materials used were carefully chosen on the basis that they were traditional, indigenous or sympathetic.

Just past the junction with the quaintly named Ticklemore Street is the little Dartmouth Inn Square, which is another good example of urban renewal. Here the pub has been refurbished, and an adjacent warehouse converted into attractive flats, which still retain the original architectural features. The Square has been re-paved, and one of Totnes's Victorian features has been introduced to act as a focal point of interest.

The Diamond Jubilee Drinking Fountain was in fact erected seven years after the event in 1904, close to the railway station by courtesy of the Great Western Railway. In its original setting on a main road into the town, it provided refreshing water for both Man and Beast. This flowed through the mouth of a dolphin before filling a trough. Such an impressive fountain obviously cost a pretty penny and the final bill for its construction was twenty-two guineas! The Jubilee fund that had been set up aimed to finance two projects, the other being a recreation ground. Alas, there

wasn't enough money, so the town settled for the fountain. This lovely feature has been preserved, and it is geologically quite interesting. Its seven-foot-square base is formed of Dartmoor Granite, and so are its four corner columns, quite probably from the famous granite quarries at Haytor. The faces are of Portland Stone, a popular material in Victorian and Edwardian times, which gives it a light and attractive appearance. The only difference from its original state is the placement of a standardised street lamp on top instead of the original circular lamp fitting. Exclusive of the lamp, it stands a statuesque twelve feet tall.

Opposite is The Chapel, which is a cleverly adapted Methodist church and former cider factory turned into flats. This sort of thing is happening quite frequently; in nearby Torquay one church has become a snooker hall and leisure centre, and another is a theatre!

At one time, a southwards walk along The Plains would have revealed one of Totnes's main imports – timber. The extensive warehouses that lined St Peter's Quay were well endowed with stocks of timber, mainly softwoods imported from Scandinavia, to serve the needs of builders' merchants throughout Devon. The Reeves Brothers, who closed in 1995, realised the potential of such an undertaking and cleverly utilised the facilities available along Totnes's many quays.

During the Second World War, Frank Curtis, a yacht builder from Looe, had been engaged at Totnes to produce 23 minesweepers and, later in the War, some 400 barges for the D-Day landings in Normandy. The adaptation of the port for the timber concern was rendered much easier as slipways and other advantages already existed.

Although most of television's *The Onedin Line* was filmed at Dartmouth or on Exeter Quay, some filming was done at Totnes. At the tip where Reeves, the Timber Merchants, dumped their sawdust, a scene was shot that demonstrates the ingenuity and deception of filmmakers, and unexpected dangers some actors have to confront from time to time. To reconstruct an erupting volcano, about ten tons of ignited sawdust were raked up and down a slope by a bulldozer whilst the actors dramatised their passing over such a dangerous obstacle. Unfortunately noxious fumes were given off, which made many of the cast ill! This is another story you can read more about in *Made in Devon*.

The town originally had no need to import timber for its buildings because the Dart Valley and immediate area was richly wooded with excellent hardwoods. Near the town were many good building stones, and quarries provided the town with a variety of materials to face the buildings and protect them from the rigours of a windy, wet climate. The Englebourne Quarry at Harbertonford, about three miles south west of Totnes, known locally as Monkey Oak, supplied slates. These were used for roofing, and also for hanging on the sides of buildings – an extra layer of protection from the elements. Most of these buildings possess rectangular slates, but some have slates cut in unusual shapes and hung in decorative patterns. Visitors will need to keep an eye open to spot them, though, as some of the better designs are above eye level. Many houses have painted their slate frontages, and the overall appearance adds life and colour to the town, though perhaps if this were 'pedestrianised' its architecture could be better appreciated.

Another common building stone in Totnes is a form of volcanic ash called tuff. This was quarried on the outskirts of the town just beyond the Dart. Although many walls and buildings are made of this, it was accepted that important buildings should be made with more substantial and durable materials. Totnes Church is a good example, with its more richly coloured red sandstone, its rock originating from the Paignton area where the sea cliffs of deep red look almost unreal. The Permian sandstones were shipped from Paignton to Totnes via coast and estuary, a distance of about 24 miles, almost four times the straight line distance between these two places. A quay was constructed near Totnes Bridge specifically for unloading the sandstone. Horses were then entrusted with the arduous task of carrying the materials up the long and steep hill to the site of the Church. Here the sandstone was used mainly in the facings.

Another stone utilised was Beer stone from the famous headland quarry in East Devon, which yielded much of the stone for Exeter Cathedral. This was also brought by sea, but a close inspection of it *in situ* may make you consider whether or not the builders should have bothered, for it appears pickled in pit marks and has worn badly.

It was trade that made Totnes Devon's second most important town in Tudor times. Strategically located on the navigable Dart, Totnes capitalised on the economic blessings so benevolently bestowed upon it by nature. The flocks of sheep on the nearby hills created an important woollen trade, whilst the herds of bovine beasts yielded sufficient hides for a leather and tanning industry of some note. The geology of the area was also kind with an abundance of Middle Devonian Slates, attractive in appearance, readily accessible and easily split for convenient use. The tin extracted on the edge of Dartmoor, probably in the vicinity of the nearest Stannary Town, Ashburton, was another important export. In the reign of Elizabeth I the town enjoyed a highly lucrative trade in pilchards. They were salted and packed in barrels in Totnes ready to tranship. If you add to these commodities all the other market produce, dairy products, meat and fish, you will begin to appreciate the town's prosperity. In later times timber and cider were added to its extensive list of trading activities. In the eighteenth century half the working population were engaged directly in farming, illustrating perhaps the significance of the town as a market centre – the Gateway to the South Hams and the Doorway to Devon.

But today the emphasis lies clearly with leisure, and for those folk who enjoy passive pleasure, a visit to Totnes's very own island provides an opportunity for some peace and quiet. For years it was simply called 'The Island' until Totnes became twinned with the Normandy town of Vire: then it became Vire Island. In the mid nineteenth century this small shady portion of land was set out as a riverside pleasure ground by a former Duke of Somerset, specifically for the enjoyment of townsfolk. There are many benches on which to sit and watch the ever-changing waterfront.

Most of the recreational activities lie on the opposite bank of the river, and to get there Totnes Bridge must be crossed. Between here and the open sea there are no bridges, except of course the ferries they call 'floating bridges' across the Dart nearer to Dartmouth. Therefore Totnes's primary importance grew as a crossing place on the river. Initially this was by a ford, a little distance above the present bridge. At low tide the water was only a few feet deep, but at high tide it was deep enough to drown a giant. A number of bridges have been built, but with changing needs they have each become inadequate. The first bridge was constructed in the time of King John and was probably wooden. Dart means oak, so this may well have been a key material. When this failed to be suitable, about 1210 a long, narrow stone bridge was built to link 'Bridgetown Pomeroy' on one side of the Dart with Totnes on the other. It is often said that this, the most dangerous piece of masonry in Devon, less than five feet wide, resembled the next bridge up river – Staverton Bridge. It was widened in 1692, but the growth in carriage and wagon traffic in the latter half of the eighteenth century rendered it unsuitable.

The present structure, built of local Devonian limestone, was designed by Charles Fowler of Exeter, and was opened in 1828. His main claim to fame was the design of Covent Garden Market in London, around the same time. He also planned Exeter's Higher and Lower Markets – the former has been adapted today to form Exeter's Guildhall Shopping Centre, and Fowler's fine columns add a touch of class to it.

However, bridges cost money and for many years travellers in South Devon were financially penalised every time they crossed it – a toll had to be paid. Fortunately for the residents of Bridgetown, the settlement just over the bridge and therefore the most inconvenienced by tolls, they would have been more independent then with their own shops and services. However, it was always regarded as a nuisance to pay; when it was announced that the tolls and the toll gates were to be abolished and demolished, there was much rejoicing in the district. October 31st 1881 was the last day that tolls had to be paid

and hardly a customer crossed the bridge that day! As midnight approached crowds gathered on both sides of the bridge. Outside the Seven Stars were two hundred excited persons assembled in eager readiness to be among the first people free to cross without the shackles of a toll. On the stroke of midnight the crowd drifted onto Totnes Bridge. The toll gates were removed to the Town Marsh where a bonfire had been prepared. As the gates were ritualistically burnt, Mr Oldrey proudly and passionately announced that this was a triumphant end to what was "a burning curse to the town." By 2.00 a.m. the crowds had gone, and so had the gates.

Now that these have gone there is free access to Bridgetown on the far bank. Today this is an integral part of Totnes, but it was once a Borough in its own right. The amount

of traffic that crosses the Dart at this point has necessitated a new road bridge a short distance upstream. Reflecting the historic legend, this has been called the Brutus Bridge, and the kindest comment that can be made is that it is functional rather than aesthetically pleasing to the eye.

In the vicinity of the Brutus Bridge, and on the south bank of the river, there used to be a venue for those who loved the Sport of Kings. There were various venues in the countryside where people would gather to watch man and beast struggle over fences and past awkward obstacles. Several of the tracks have gone, and the Totnes race track is now buried beneath an industrial estate.

Large crowds gathered for this important event on the Totnes calendar of the past. An old newspaper article revealed that on September 3rd and 4th in 1834 racing would take place on the banks of the Dart just upstream of Totnes Bridge. If you wanted to register your horse for the first day's racing you had to do so at Webb's Hotel, but if it was for the second day you had to go to the Seymour Hotel. In both instances Samuel Heath accepted the entries. Racing ran strictly to time with 'the off' at 1.00 p.m. sharp. It was clearly stated that any dogs found on the course would be immediately destroyed! The steeplechases involved a spectacular race that crossed the Dart twice, but on one occasion there was a miscalculation as to the state of the tide in the river, it being higher and the river deeper than anticipated. The resulting chaos and confusion gave the enormous crowd something to talk about all the way home. There were some very sorry scenes as bedraggled riders and horses made their way back. It is believed that no man nor beast came to any great harm in that particular Somerset Steeplechase.

Racing began at Totnes in 1785, and, despite lapses, survived until 1939 when the Admiralty requisitioned the race marsh. The Americans used the banks of the Dart to build barges for the D-Day landings, so after the war the ground was unsuitable for racing.

The Totnes race course encircled another important local amenity, the Totnes Golf Course. This too now lies beneath a trading estate, but it had nine holes and was almost 2,000 yards long. According to the 1931 Guide, Sunday play was only permitted after 2.00 p.m.

Just beyond Totnes Bridge is an attractive building, which was formerly the Seymour Hotel. It was built in 1832 by the Duke of Somerset, and had a ballroom added in the twentieth century. As has been the case with many hotels in Devon, this one has been converted into flats.

On a fine summer's day, the Steamer Quay on the side of the river is a place of hustle and bustle with people enjoying the river.

Just outside Totnes the River Dart is joined by a small tributary called the River Hems, which gives its name to quietly beautiful villages such as Broadhempston and Littlehempston. The valleys of both the Dart and the Hems have provided a natural corridor for railway routes. The main line from Exeter to Plymouth runs southwards towards the town along the latter.

In 1847 the coming of the railways to Totnes did not improve the town's economic prosperity, if anything it simply managed to result in a great reduction of river trade. Unlike the nearby resort towns of Dawlish, Teignmouth, Torquay and Paignton, the population of Totnes did not rise greatly. Brunel was the engineer for the South Devon Railway's route from Exeter onwards towards Cornwall. He favoured an Atmospheric System, which meant that Pumping Houses were built every three miles along the line. Unfortunately, although his idea was excellent, breakdowns were so frequent that the system was abandoned in favour of a more conventional form of locomotion. There was a typical atmospheric pumping house built beside the present Totnes station, but it was never used for its intended purpose, and for many years it has served the area in the dairy industry. However, Totnes was not deterred by Brunel's initial failure, and the station became a showpiece with attractive flower beds and palm trees lining the platforms, just the ticket for someone arriving at the end of a long journey.

In 1872 a branch line was extended up the Dart Valley to Ashburton. The little engine which plied this line was fondly nicknamed 'Bulliver' by locals, but the great railway 'axe' of the late 1950s and early 60s saw many lines like this close down all over the country. This line ceased operation in 1958. However, railway enthusiasts refused to

give in and, after much negotiation and even more toil and sweat, the Dart Valley Railway line opened from Buckfastleigh to run almost into Totnes. The first section of this branch line from Ashburton to Buckfastleigh is lost beneath the A38 Exeter to Plymouth road, but the rest of the line to Totnes is still there to be enjoyed. Passengers alighting from the steam trains at 'Totnes Riverside' can cross the Dart to enjoy a visit to the ancient town. Today the line is called the South Devon Railway.

The ride through the valley is beautiful and it's a journey well worth doing. The level crossing at Staverton Mill is called 'Knapper's Crossing' after Mrs. Knapper, a well loved and highly respected lady who operated the crossing gates for many years.

So far we have not mentioned the obvious journey that most visitors make when visiting Totnes, and that is to take the down river trip on one of the many river passenger ferries, which ply their way down the twelve miles to Dartmouth. This seventy-five minute journey is by far the best way to get from Totnes to Dartmouth, a voyage of great beauty with plenty to see. The ferry operators are all experts on the moods and ways of the river, and they have evolved their own historical and geographical patter, which will educate and no doubt amuse you.

Do keep an eye open for the impressive Sharpham House, the beautiful village of Stoke Gabriel, the inlet of Bow Creek, the waterside settlement of Dittisham, and the Anchor Stone (the Dart's equivalent of the Lorelei Rock). The journey also passes Agatha Christie's former hideaway, Greenway House, and eventually reaches the Royal Naval College at Dartmouth. For the lover of wildlife and great scenery, there is so much to see, so have a good voyage! A permanent souvenir of such a journey is another of my books, *Down the Dart–Boat Trip Totnes to Dartmouth*.

If you are a dedicated landlubber, you may prefer to remain on terra firma, and if it's terror you are looking for, then a visit to Berry Pomeroy Castle may be just the thing, as it is reputedly one of the most haunted castles in England! Berry Pomeroy Castle lies about two miles to the north-east of Totnes. It is an ancient building sited on the side of a steep slope high above the Gatcombe Brook, a tributary of the Hems, which we've already said flows into the Dart on the edge of Totnes. An excellent little book called *The Ghosts of Berry Pomeroy Castle* by Deryck Seymour will tell you all about its haunted happenings.

No visit to this area would be complete without a slight detour to Bowden House, which lies about a mile from the centre of Totnes. It is well signposted from the A381 Totnes–Kingsbridge road, and precise details of opening times can be found at tourist information centres, or from the house itself.

My first visit was out of season, a rain-lashed late Autumn night, to be involved in an ITV documentary about Berry Pomeroy Castle. With a blazing fire, excellent food and wine and surfeit of good company, it was easy for the assembled crowd to relate their ghostly experiences as the cameras rolled in such a convivial atmosphere.

In mediaeval times Bowden was the home of the Lords of the Manor of Totnes. Changes of ownership have been numerous; for a while it was the property of the Black Canons, being the perfect place to pray, meditate or simply develop good habits. In the 1520s the house was converted into a Tudor brick mansion, a reflection of the great wealth of John Giles, who was reputedly not only the richest man in Devon, but also one of the most generous and caring, looking after many impoverished folk in hard times. However, it was Nicholas Trist who bought Bowden in 1704, and who added the Queen Anne façade that gives the house its distinctly symmetrical appearance today. Nicholas

The Great Little Totnes Book

had two grandsons who found their way to America. One of them, also a Nicholas, bought land in Louisiana, but died of the fever. The other grandson, Hoare-Browse Trist, survived and his family found fame and fortune. It is believed that they once purchased an area of Western America that was about 350 times the size of Devon, or six times that of England! California made up a substantial segment of this 'modest' acquisition.

Paris Singer, one of the Singer Family famous for their sewing machines, had settled at Oldway Mansion at Paignton. He saw a need for a stud farm, and duly purchased Bowden for a snip. An extremely large adjoining field was ideal, almost tailor-made, for exercising the horses, and race meetings were occasionally held there.

Like most large houses in Devon, Bowden, in time of war, was commandeered for military purposes. At various times British, Canadian and American troops all could be found camped in Bowden's grounds. The Americans took over six South Hams parishes for their D-Day preparations, and Bowden was ideally sited on the fringe of the frenzied and fatal activities that could be heard in the distance.

Bowden lies close to the edge of Totnes Parish, and from time to time the age old practice of circumnavigating the town is executed with great adventure and fun. In September 1905 the old tradition of 'Beating the Bounds' in Totnes was rekindled after a lapse of some 14 years. The Mayor, Captain Adams RN, had felt that it was about time that the limits of the town should be perambulated. After all, since the last time, new lands had been added to create a larger and more important 'Greater Totnes' with an area of 1,170 acres.

About 150 citizens gathered, many of them schoolboys celebrating an extra day off school specifically granted for the event. The mood and atmosphere of the 'bounders' was particularly jovial, and when they set off there was an enormous expectation of fun and frolicking. In the first mile, after traversing Race Marsh, the River Dart had to be crossed at Seymour Hutch. Despite having several boats ready to ferry the participants across the River, many succumbed to a soaking and a poor lad called Foster fell in. At the first bond stone the Mayor gave the bumps to another boy, and the Dart was duly re-crossed. At Tibbicombe Head's bond stone an acrobatic boy climbed onto the bond stone and stood on his head for several seconds amidst the throng. By now the wanderers had worked up an appetite, so at Eagle Quarry refreshments were made available; as an additional entertainment, the Mayor threw coins for the boys to frantically scramble and fight over. The way ahead saw the throng pass Bowden, Standcombe and the Gerston Estate to reach Peeke Cross. At this spot the Mayor set them off on a series of athletic races. At Cholwell Cross poor old John Hill fell from a high hedge and broke his wrist. After Follaton the assembly followed the line of the Cholwell Brook; by staying on the river banks, they soon reached Malt Mills. The company were now tiring somewhat and the climb up Barracks Hill, and eventually to the two bond stones beyond Redworth, took its toll. The surveyor's son, called W. W. Tollit, was bumped by the Mayor, and seeing Master F. Weymouth laugh unduly, gave him the bumps himself. By following the Bidwell Brook the ensemble reached Totnes Weir, the circuit now almost complete. In a state of mild exhaustion, the Mayor made an entertaining little speech where he outlined, jokingly, his hope that the ancient borough of Totnes should not seek to enlarge its boundaries any further. The six-hour long expedition ended on The Plains, where cheers were given for both the King and the Mayor.

We have seen in this little book that Totnes is far from being a dull place, and certainly not just a sleepy little Elizabethan town. Totnes does indeed have a particular vitality in its trade, in its shops and along its waterfront. The Dart is an important feature in Totnes life, and we have only considered a very short part of a river, which was dubbed by Queen Victoria 'The English Rhine'. To the north lies its most attractive man-made feature.

Staverton Bridge is, as the crow flies, a few miles to the north-north-west of Totnes, and is about three quarters of a mile from Dartington. It lies a short distance from the A384 Buckfastleigh to Totnes road. This smart stone bridge probably dates back to 1314, so for nearly seven centuries the waters of the Dart have passed beneath its seven arches. The next crossing place is almost three miles downstream at Totnes.

The river is not always peaceful: when in flood, it is an awesome spectacle. On 17th August 1840 John Edmunds was married at Staverton Church, but within hours was drowned, along with his new wife, when a great wall of water swept them away to watery deaths. Her body was found shortly afterwards, but his was not discovered for almost three weeks. The horse was carried right down beyond Totnes Weir, such was the might of the torrent. The Dart is known as a cruel river – a well-known and much overused rhyming couplet relates the message that the river claims a heart at least once a year, every year, and thus commands great respect from its many users. At the time of the Edmunds' untimely deaths, Staverton was a thriving village with many of its population being gainfully employed at the mill. In 1851 the village had a population of 1,152 which is almost double that of today's figure.

One of the village's attractions is the Sea Trout Inn, which until about 1957 was called, like many inns in South Devon, the Church House Inn. The many fine sea trout in the Dart inspired a change of name. The pub is a cottage-style building, and dates back to the fifteenth century when it was owned by the church. It was used as a resting house for monks whilst they were taking time out from building Buckfast Abbey – the first one on that site, and not the one you see today as that was only finished in 1938!

Picturesque Staverton Bridge Station has been used as a location for many television programmes and films, so if you are visiting for the first time and you get the feeling of *déjà-vu*, it may be explained away quite simply in that you have probably seen it numerous times on television! Once again, more details can be found in *Made in Devon*!

The river and railway are obliged to pass around the great hill of Dartington in their quest to reach Totnes. If the oldest buildings at Dartington could talk they would be able to relate stories ranging from the toils of everyday endeavour right through to sensational scandals. Dartington is one of the oldest settlements in Devon and dates back to Saxon times. It is located on a steeply rising, south-east facing, slope above the River Dart. The river does a gigantic loop around Dartington on its way from Staverton to Totnes. First it runs almost north-east before turning south-west below Dartington. On this relatively small area of land great men have thought great thoughts and great artists have been inspired to great works of art – it's that sort of place!

Eight generations of Martins held the lands from the early twelfth century onwards, but the lands reverted to the Crown in 1384 with Richard II's violent half brother John Holland, who was later Duke of Exeter, being the fortunate recipient. Dartington Hall became his principal seat in Devon, and the spectacular great Hall dates from this time.

The Champernownes appeared on the scene in the sixteenth century, and held on to the manor until the twentieth century. However, at the end of their reign there was much evidence that parts of the estate had become ruinous. By 1925 most of its 1,000 acres of fine farmland had become derelict, and the great Hall was a roofless ruin. Archdeacon Froude had the roof removed, as it was unsafe. Salvaged from it was enough timber to enable altars to be made at churches in Holne, Dartington and Ottery St Mary.

The transformation that took place after the Elmhirsts bought it in September 1925 is something of a fairy tale, although in this particular instance it was not fairies but vision and industry that brought about such a dramatic change. Leonard and Dorothy Elmhirst acknowledged the loveliness of the surroundings, and agreed that it was the perfect place for children to grow up. Their school started with nine pupils, the offspring of enlightened folk who appreciated that there is more to learning than a classroom with four walls populated by traditional scholarly schoolmasters. The 'teachers' did other things on the estate – a textile mill clothed one plot of land, whilst words cannot convey the excitement of the Dance-Mime Studio that was created. The Dartington Trust was established in 1931, and its activities have covered a wide spectrum. In 1936 they had the foresight to introduce apple juice to England. In 1944 they took the bull by the horns (for want of a better phrase) and became pioneers in the field of artificial insemination in Devon. This greatly reduced the number of farms requiring bulls of their own, which, in turn, no doubt reduced the stress level for ramblers traversing through fields!

However, it is in a different type of field that Dartington has made its name, and that is the field of the Arts and Crafts. The name is synonymous with skill and quality, the lasting fruits of the seeds sown by the Elmhirsts all those years ago. The influence of the Dartington revival has spread far and wide. R. C. Sherriff, of Totnes ancestry, spent a holiday at an inn at Ringmore, near Bigbury Bay, and in the 1920s wrote a play called *Journey's End*. The Elmhirsts financed the West End production of it. The inn has since changed its name to that of the play's title, and for anyone staying in the Totnes area, it is a pleasant drive to visit it.

There is great beauty in and around the grounds at Dartington, and its secrets and treasures are there to be discovered. The little bronze donkey is just one in a box of delights. It was fashioned by Willi Soukop, an Austrian, who came to England in 1934, and was at Dartington for a long while. This beautiful creation was made for the Chelsea Flower Show. It proved so popular that you may chance to come across its brothers or sisters that were commissioned to adorn the landscape of Leicestershire: there is even one at Harlow New Town.

Quality seems to be the hallmark of everything that goes on in and around Dartington. The Cider Press Centre at Shinners Bridge is one of the biggest conglomerations of gift shops in the region. Dartington Glass products, ornaments, pottery, cloth items, fragrances and all manner of gifts are on display.

And so we come to the end of our brief look around Totnes, and its immediate neighbourhood. We have climbed its steep and narrow streets, and have heard many tales, but have still only touched on a handful of its historic happenings, so steeped is it in a long and interesting history. We hope you have enjoyed this light-hearted little book, and we trust that it provides the perfect picture and souvenir of the lovely and, dare we say, unique, town of Totnes.

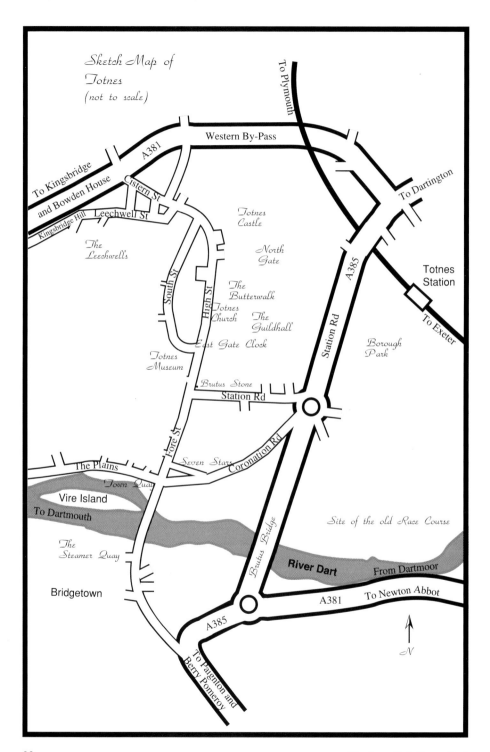

Sketch Map of Totnes
(not to scale)

To Plymouth

Western By-Pass

A381

To Kingsbridge and Bowden House

Cistern St

Kingsbridge Hill

Leechwell St

The Leechwells

South St

High St

Totnes Castle

North Gate

The Butterwalk

Totnes Church

The Guildhall

East Gate Clock

Totnes Museum

Brutus Stone

Station Rd

Station Rd

A385

Totnes Station

To Dartington

To Exeter

Borough Park

Fore St

Seven Stars

Coronation Rd

The Plains

Town Quay

Vire Island

To Dartmouth

The Steamer Quay

Bridgetown

Brutus Bridge

River Dart

Site of the old Race Course

From Dartmoor

A381

To Newton Abbot

A385

To Paignton and Berry Pomeroy

N